MORNING RIDE

by Adam Porter

Illustrated by Alyssa Whetstone

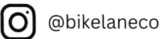 @bikelaneco

www.thebikelaneco.com

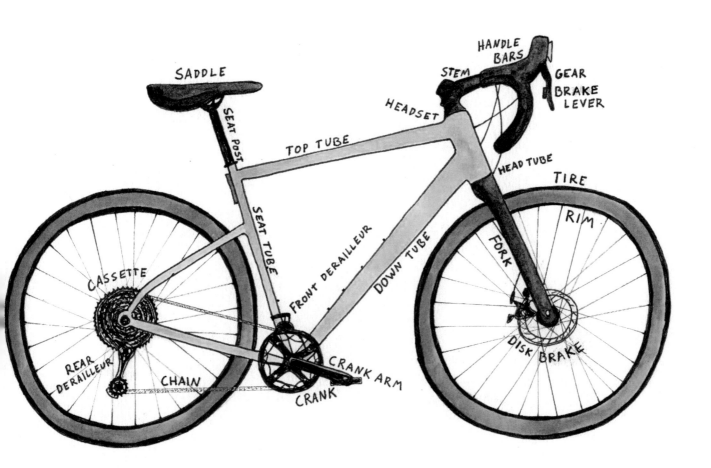

Today is a great day for a ride. The sky is dark and cloudy, and everyone is still asleep. All the essential gear is packed and ready to go, including a cold water bottle, a charged bike computer, and bright headlights and tail lights. With a quick clip-in to the pedals, it's time to hit the road.

The neighborhood is calm and quiet. The rocking chairs on the porch of the brown house are ready for sitting and sipping morning tea.

Pedaling faster makes the cold morning air rush against your cheeks, nose, and ears. The tree house is empty for now, but will soon be filled with sword fights, secret clubs, and maybe a peanut butter and jelly sandwich lunch.

Landscapers arrive in their blue short-bed pickup truck and begin to unload their equipment. The next part of the ride is out of the neighborhood and onto the trail ahead.

The ride is now off the smooth street and has jumped on to the gravel trail. The soft quiet sounds of the neighborhood's birds chirping, or the musical tones of windchimes rustling is now taken over by the sound of chunky tires rolling over the dirt and crunching on loose rocks, both big and small.

A few younger trees are eager for the morning sun's warmth to help them grow taller like their neighbors. The trail quickly heads upward. The view at the top is well worth the tough miles of uphill pedaling.

The sun is now peeking through the clouds, hills, and trees. It casts light on the trail below, brightening the rocks and grass in the field.

The end of the uphill climb is in sight! After all the hard work, a quick break and a moment to enjoy the bright sunrise view is just ahead.

SPEED
0 MPH
DISTANCE
8.1 mi
ELEVATION
1401 ft

With a tight grip on the handlebars, the bike hurtles from the top of the mountain down the trail, navigating sharp turns and rattling over rough terrain. Finally, the tires meet smooth pavement again.

Volleyball players rake the sand smooth, stretch their tanned arms and legs, and set up the net. A full day in the sun of bumping, setting, and spiking are ahead of them.

Every good morning ride needs a coffee and breakfast burrito stop. Scrambled eggs and crispy potatoes with salsa is the ideal meal to fuel-up for the ride back. The sound of waves crashing at the shore behind the cafe is the perfect soundtrack to breakfast.

Shoppers and beachgoers begin to fill the sidewalks. A girl in a green tie-dye shirt peeks into the bookstore window, pointing out colorful books on trains, surfing, farm animals, and many others.

The bike's derailers click and shift into the best pedaling speed for the flat, straight stretch of gravel road ahead. The handlebars shake and rattle from the bumps and rocks on the trail.

Cars zoom by, heading for beach adventures. Meanwhile, above the sparkling waters, birds glide effortlessly, their eyes trained on the waves below, hoping for a morning catch of fish to start their day.

The ride is now off the highway and back on to a dirt road heading toward home. Down the long driveway of the lone blue cottage, a carefully planted flower field is in full bloom, with bright colors of red, pink, yellow, and purple standing out against the green field.

A sudden jolt, followed by a slight slipping feeling and rattling thuds, means that a sharp rock has punctured and flattened the rear tire.

The repaired tire has continued to hold air allowing for a safe journey back to the neighborhood.

The landscapers have finished their work. Toys are scattered around
the tree house from a morning of play.

The final few pushes of the pedals bring the trip to an end.

Back home now, but already thinking about the adventures of the next morning ride.

SPEED	AVERAGE SPEED
0 MPH	15.4
MOVING TIME	DISTANCE
1:43:08	22.1 mi
ELEVATION	CALORIES
1503 ft	765

ABOUT THE AUTHOR

Adam Porter is a husband and proud dad of five children, from Mesa, Arizona. He is a rider and collector of vintage bikes. Inspired by his own morning rides, Adam wrote this book to help fellow cyclists share their love of riding with their kids.

thebikelaneco.com
@bikelaneco

ABOUT THE ILLUSTRATOR

Alyssa Whetstone is an artist and art teacher from Minnesota who uses pen and watercolor to represent the world around her. She is often inspired by real places and hopes each viewer feels a sense of comfort and joy when they see her artwork.

Learn more by finding her online.
alyssawhetstoneart.com
@alyssawhetstoneart

Thank you for reading Morning Ride! If you loved reading it as much as we loved creating it, please leave a review on Amazon and share with a friend! Your review helps others discover our books about bikes!

Check out this additional book from Bike Lane Co.

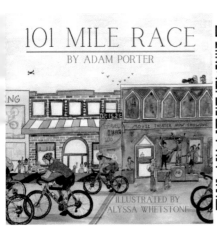

Join in for a 101 mile long bike race! Watch out for stormy weather as you race from the starting line all the way to the finish line.

Made in United States
Troutdale, OR
12/08/2024